LIFE'S LITTLE BOOK OF WISDOM FOR
Husbands

Published by Barbour Publishing, Inc., P.O. Box 719, Uhrichsville, Ohio 44683, www.barbourbooks.com

Our mission is to publish and distribute inspirational products offering exceptional value and biblical encouragement to the masses.

 Member of the
Evangelical Christian
Publishers Association

Printed in China.

LIFE'S LITTLE BOOK OF
WISDOM FOR
Husbands

BARBOUR
PUBLISHING

It is by loving, and not by being loved,
that one can come nearest
the soul of another.

GEORGE MacDONALD

Love does not delight in evil
but rejoices with the truth.

1 CORINTHIANS 13:6 NIV

So long as we love, we serve.

ROBERT LOUIS STEVENSON

The love of a family is life's greatest blessing.

UNKNOWN

The heart is wiser than the intellect.

JOSIAH HOLLAND

The invariable mark of wisdom is
to see the miraculous in the common.

RALPH WALDO EMERSON

The six most important words:
I admit I made a mistake.
The five most important words:
You did a good job.
The four most important words:
What is your opinion?
The three most important words:
If you please.
The two most important words: Thank you.
The one least important word: I.

ANONYMOUS

Great works do not always lie in our way,
but every moment we may do little ones
excellently, that is, with great love.

FRANCIS DE SALES

Faith, like light, should always be simple
and unbending; while love, like warmth,
should beam forth on every side
and bend to every necessity.

MARTIN LUTHER

It is the heart that makes a man rich.
He is rich according to what he is,
not according to what he has.

HENRY WARD BEECHER

Patience is the companion of wisdom.

AUGUSTINE

Men acquire a particular quality
by constantly acting a particular way. . . .
You become just by performing just actions,
temperate by performing temperate actions,
brave by performing brave actions.

ARISTOTLE

Let love be genuine. . .
hold fast to what is good;
love one another with mutual affection;
outdo one another in showing honor.

ROMANS 12:9-10 NRSV

No legacy is so rich as honesty.

WILLIAM SHAKESPEARE

Expecting is the greatest impediment to living.
In anticipation of tomorrow, it loses today.

SENECA

Caring is the greatest thing.
Caring matters most.

FRIEDRICH VON HÜGEL

Is life not full of opportunities for
learning love? Every man and woman
every day has a thousand of them. . . .
And the one eternal lesson for us all
is how better we can love.

HENRY DRUMMOND

Be sincere and true to your word,
serious and careful in your actions.

CONFUCIUS

Don't judge each day by
the harvest you reap,
but by the seeds you plant.

ROBERT LOUIS STEVENSON

The best portion of a good man's life
is his little, nameless, unremembered
acts of kindness and of love.

WILLIAM WORDSWORTH

For faith to be true, it has to be generous and loving. Love and faith go together; they complete each other.

MOTHER TERESA

Whoever pursues righteousness and
kindness will find life and honor.

PROVERBS 21:21 NRSV

I would rather be able to appreciate things
I cannot have than to have things
I am not able to appreciate.

ELBERT HUBBARD

While faith makes all things possible,
it is love that makes all things easy.

GERARD MANLEY HOPKINS

What the heart has once owned and had,
it shall never lose.

HENRY WARD BEECHER

The test. . .is not whether our commitments
match our will and our courage,
but whether we have the will and courage
to match our commitments.

LYNDON B. JOHNSON

In a moment of decision, the best thing
you can do is the right thing to do.
The worst thing you can do is nothing.

THEODORE ROOSEVELT

Be faithful in small things,
because it is in them that your strength lies.

MOTHER TERESA

Faith supplies staying power.

Norman Vincent Peale

Often we can help each other most
by leaving each other alone;
at other times we need the hand-grasp
and the word of cheer.

ELBERT HUBBARD

To every thing there is a season,
and a time to every purpose under the heaven. . . .
A time to embrace. . . . A time to love.

ECCLESIASTES 3:1, 5, 8 KJV

Life is short, and we never have
enough time for gladdening the hearts
of those who travel the way with us.
Oh, be swift to love! Make haste to be kind.

HENRI-FRÉDÉRIC AMIEL

Life's lasting joy
comes in erasing the
boundary line between
"mine" and "yours."

UNKNOWN

Where does the family start?
It starts with a young man
falling in love with a girl—
no superior alternative has yet been found.

WINSTON CHURCHILL

A kiss makes the heart young
again and wipes out the years.

Rupert Brooke

The right word may be effective,
but no word was ever as effective
as a rightly timed pause.

MARK TWAIN

Kindness is more than deeds.
It is an attitude, an expression, a look, a touch.
It is anything that lifts another person.

UNKNOWN

To love anyone is nothing else
than to wish that person good.

THOMAS AQUINAS

Be completely humble and gentle;
be patient, bearing with one another in love.

EPHESIANS 4:2 NIV

Whatever a man's actions are, such must be his spirit.

DEMOSTHENES

'Tis the most tender part of love,
each other to forgive.

JOHN SHEFFIELD

Spread love everywhere you go:
first of all in your own house. . . .
Let no one ever come to you without
leaving better and happier.
Be the living expression of God's kindness:
kindness in your face, kindness in your eyes,
kindness in your smile.

MOTHER TERESA

Where we love is home,
home that our feet may leave,
but not our hearts.

OLIVER WENDELL HOLMES

We can only love what we know,
and we can never know completely
what we do not love.

UNKNOWN

There are two sorts of affection—
the love of a woman you respect,
and the love for the woman you love.

Arthur Wing Pinero

The first duty of love is to listen.

PAUL TILLICH

Be gentle with one another, sensitive.
Forgive one another as quickly and thoroughly
as God in Christ forgave you.

EPHESIANS 4:32 MSG

A great wife, kids, and health
are a man's greatest wealth.

UNKNOWN

Love is saying, "I feel differently,"
instead of "You're wrong."

UNKNOWN

Whenever you're in conflict with someone,
there is one factor that can make the
difference between damaging your
relationship and deepening it.
That factor is attitude.

WILLIAM JAMES

Respect is love in plain clothes.

FRANKIE BYRNE

Love is everything. It is the key of life,
and its influences are those that move the world.

RALPH WALDO EMERSON

To worship rightly is to love each other,
each smile a hymn, each kindly deed a prayer.

JOHN GREENLEAF WHITTIER

A successful marriage requires
falling in love many times,
always with the same person.

MIGNON McLAUGHLIN

God is love.

1 JOHN 4:16 NIV

A good marriage is one which allows
for change and growth in the individuals
and in the way they express their love.

PEARL S. BUCK

Remember that if thou marry for beauty,
thou bindest thyself all thy life for that which
perchance will neither last nor please thee one year;
and when thou hast it, it will be to thee of no price
at all; for the desire dieth when it is attained,
and the affection perisheth when it is satisfied.

WALTER RALEIGH

Learning to live in the present
moment is part of the path of joy.

SARAH BAN BREATHNACH

Courtesies of a small and trivial character
are the ones which strike deepest in the
grateful and appreciating heart.

HENRY CLAY

Feelings of worth can flourish
only in an atmosphere where individual
differences are appreciated, mistakes are tolerated,
communication is open, and rules are flexible.

VIRGINIA SATIR

All love that has not friendship
for its base is like a mansion
built upon the sand.

ELLA WHEELER WILCOX

Love can hope where
reason would despair.

GEORGE LYTTELTON

Agree with one another, live in peace;
and the God of love and peace will be with you.

2 CORINTHIANS 13:11 NRSV

The ultimate measure of a man is
not where he stands in moments of comfort
and convenience, but where he stands in times
of challenge and controversy.

MARTIN LUTHER KING JR.

The art of life is to live in the present moment and to make that moment as perfect as we can by the realization that we are the instruments and expression of God Himself.

EMMET FOX

True happiness is. . .to enjoy the present,
without anxious dependence upon the future.

SENECA

Forgive, forget. Bear with the faults of others
as you would have them bear with yours.
Be patient and understanding.

PHILLIPS BROOKS

Love is never afraid of giving too much.

UNKNOWN

Good company on a journey
makes the way seem shorter.

Izaak Walton

It's difficult to imagine anything more nourishing to the soul than family life.

THOMAS MORE

Love others as you love yourself.

GALATIANS 5:14 MSG

Take one thing with another,
and the world is a pretty good sort of a world,
and it is our duty to make the best of it,
and be thankful.

BENJAMIN FRANKLIN

Comfort and prosperity have never enriched
the world as much as adversity has.
Out of pain and problems have come the
sweetest songs, and the most gripping stories.

BILLY GRAHAM

It is in giving that we receive.

FRANCIS OF ASSISI

Flowers leave their fragrance
on the hand that bestows them.

CHINESE PROVERB

Blessed is the influence of one true,
loving human soul on another.

George Eliot

Each of us makes his own weather,
determines the color of the skies in the
emotional universe which he inhabits.

FULTON J. SHEEN

Courage is what it takes to stand up and speak.
Courage is also what it takes to sit down and listen.

WINSTON CHURCHILL

Husbands, go all out in your love for your wives,
exactly as Christ did for the church—
a love marked by giving, not getting.

EPHESIANS 5:25 MSG

The true measure of loving...
is to love without measure.

BERNARD OF CLAIRVAUX

Have a purpose in life and, having it,
throw such strength of mind and muscle
into your work as God has given you.

THOMAS CARLYLE

We cannot tell what may happen to us
in the strange medley of life.
But we can decide what happens in us—
how we take it, what we do with it—
and that is what really counts in the end.

JOSEPH FORT NEWTON

The world is a looking glass and gives back
to every man the reflection of his own face.

WILLIAM MAKEPEACE THACKERAY

Love is never lost.
If not reciprocated, it will flow back
and soften and purify the heart.

WASHINGTON IRVING

Love doesn't try to see through the loved one,
but to see the loved one through.

UNKNOWN

Where love is, God is also.

LEO TOLSTOY

Above all, love each other deeply,
because love covers over
a multitude of sins.

1 PETER 4:8 NIV

Bring love into your home, for this is
where our love for each other must start.

MOTHER TERESA

Let God love you through others, and let God love others through you.

D. M. STREET

He who reigns within himself and rules
passions, desires, and fears is more than a king.

JOHN MILTON

We must learn to let go, to give up,
to make room for the things
we have prayed for and desired.

CHARLES FILLMORE

Favorite people, favorite places,
favorite memories of the past—
These are the joys of a lifetime;
these are the things that last.

HENRY VAN DYKE

Love is the highest gift of God.
All of our revelations and gifts are
little things compared to love.

JOHN WESLEY

Love does not consist in gazing
at each other but in looking outward
together in the same direction.

ANTOINE DE SAINT-EXUPÉRY

Riches take wings, comfort vanishes,
hope withers away, but love stays with us.
God is love.

LEW WALLACE

Enjoy the wife you married as a young man!
Lovely as an angel, beautiful as a rose. . . .
Never take her love for granted!

PROVERBS 5:18-19 MSG

You don't love a woman because she is beautiful,
but she is beautiful because you love her.

UNKNOWN

Real love is the universal language—
understood by all.

HENRY DRUMMOND

We are not meant to be seen as God's perfect,
bright-shining examples, but to be seen as
the everyday essence of ordinary lives
exhibiting the miracle of His grace.

OSWALD CHAMBERS

When you love someone,
you love the whole person, just as he or she is,
and not as you would like them to be.

LEO TOLSTOY

A man is not where he lives,
but where he loves.

LATIN PROVERB

There is nothing nobler or more admirable
than when two people who see eye to eye
keep house as man and wife.

HOMER

You can give without loving,
but you cannot love without giving.

AMY CARMICHAEL

Love is like a violin.
The music may stop now and then,
but the strings remain forever.

UNKNOWN

Owe no one anything,
except to love one another.

ROMANS 13:8 NRSV

We cannot really love anybody
with whom we never laugh.

AGNES REPPLIER

Every single act of love bears the imprint of God.

UNKNOWN

Love gives itself; it is not bought.

HENRY WADSWORTH LONGFELLOW

The purpose of life is not to be happy.
It is to be useful, to be honorable,
to be compassionate, to have it make
some difference that you have
lived and lived well.

RALPH WALDO EMERSON

You cannot make yourself feel something
you do not feel, but you can make yourself
do right in spite of your feelings.

PEARL S. BUCK

Perhaps the greatest social service that can be
rendered by anybody to this country and
to mankind is to bring up a family.

GEORGE BERNARD SHAW

Love is patient, love is kind. It does not envy,
it does not boast, it is not proud. It is not rude,
it is not self-seeking, it is not easily angered,
it keeps no record of wrongs.

1 CORINTHIANS 13:4-5 NIV

There is no duty we so underrate as the duty of being happy. By being happy we sow anonymous benefits upon the world.

ROBERT LOUIS STEVENSON

Let us be grateful to people who make us happy;
they are the charming gardeners who
make our souls blossom.

MARCEL PROUST

Love is a great thing, an altogether good gift,
the only thing that makes burdens light
and bears all that is hard with ease.
It carries a weight without feeling it
and makes all that is bitter
sweet and pleasant to the taste.

THOMAS À KEMPIS

Do not forget little kindnesses,
and do not remember small faults.

CHINESE PROVERB

A good heart is better than all the heads in the world.

Edward Bulwer-Lytton

When you have once seen the glow
of happiness on the face of a beloved person,
you know that a man can have no vocation
but to awaken that light on the
faces surrounding him.

ALBERT CAMUS

The life I touch for good or ill
will touch another life, and that in turn
another, until who knows where the
trembling stops or in what far place
my touch will be felt.

FREDERICK BUECHNER

Trust steadily in God,
hope unswervingly, love extravagantly.
And the best of the three is love.

1 CORINTHIANS 13:13 MSG

It's faith in something and
enthusiasm for something that
makes a life worth living.

OLIVER WENDELL HOLMES

There is no beautifier of complexion,
or form, or behavior, like the wish
to scatter joy and not pain around us.

RALPH WALDO EMERSON

With each day, love brings new hope
and enthusiasm for every shared tomorrow.

UNKNOWN

Love is a fabric that never fades,
no matter how often it is washed in
the waters of adversity and grief.

UNKNOWN

We are healed of a suffering only
by expressing it to the full.

MARCEL PROUST

Whoso loves, believes the impossible.

ELIZABETH BARRETT BROWNING

Happiness cannot come from without. It must come from within. It is not what we see and touch or that which others do for us which makes us happy; it is that which we think and feel and do, first for the other fellow and then for ourselves.

HELEN KELLER

Go after a life of love
as if your life depended on it—
because it does.

1 CORINTHIANS 14:1 MSG

Always set high value on spontaneous kindness.

SAMUEL JOHNSON

Love is a circle—
the more you give, the more comes around.

UNKNOWN

The rewards of love are always greater than its cost.

UNKNOWN

We need not think alike to love alike.

Francis David

Love seems the swiftest,
but it is the slowest of all growths.

MARK TWAIN

Only two things are necessary to keep
one's wife happy. One is to let her think
she is having her own way,
and the other is to let her have it.

LYNDON B. JOHNSON

Observe how Christ loved us.
His love was not cautious but extravagant.
He didn't love in order to get something from us
but to give everything of himself to us.
Love like that.

EPHESIANS 5:2 MSG

My advice to you is to get married.
If you find a good wife, you'll be happy.

SOCRATES

Chains do not hold a marriage together.
It is threads, hundreds of tiny threads which
sew people together through the years.
That is what makes a marriage last.

SIMONE SIGNORET

Love is not love, which alters
when it alteration finds.

WILLIAM SHAKESPEARE

Familiar acts are beautiful through love.

PERCY BYSSHE SHELLEY

To keep your marriage brimming
with love in the loving cup,
whenever you're wrong admit it;
whenever you're right shut up.

OGDEN NASH

One moment of patience may ward off great disaster. One moment of impatience may ruin a whole life.

CHINESE PROVERB

We are here on earth
to do good for others.

W. H. AUDEN

Never forget that the purpose for which a man lives is the improvement of the man himself, so that he may go out of this world having, in his great sphere or his small one, done some little good for his fellow creatures and labored a little to diminish the sin and sorrow that are in the world.

WILLIAM E. GLADSTONE

The fruit of the Spirit is love, joy, peace, patience, kindness, goodness, faithfulness, gentleness and self-control.

GALATIANS 5:22-23 NIV

Try not to become a man of success,
but rather try to become a man of value.

ALBERT EINSTEIN

The happiness of life is made up of minute fractions—the little, soon-forgotten charities of a kiss or a smile, a kind look, or heartfelt compliment.

Samuel Taylor Coleridge

Love is most divine when it loves
according to needs and not
according to merit.

GEORGE MACDONALD

We cannot live for ourselves alone.
Our lives are connected by a thousand
invisible threads, and along these
sympathetic fibers, our actions run
as causes and return to us as results.

HERMAN MELVILLE

If you will think about what you
ought to do for other people,
your character will take care of itself.

WOODROW WILSON

Nothing is so strong as gentleness,
nothing so gentle as real strength.

FRANCIS DE SALES

We know the truth, not only by the reason, but also by the heart.

BLAISE PASCAL

Don't lose your grip on Love and Loyalty.
Tie them around your neck;
carve their initials on your heart.
Earn a reputation for living well.

PROVERBS 3:3-4 MSG

Treat people as if they were what
they ought to be, and you help them
to become what they are capable of being.

JOHANN WOLFGANG VON GOETHE

Life in abundance comes
only through great love.

ELBERT HUBBARD

To love is to place our happiness
in the happiness of another.

GOTTFRIED WILHELM VON LIEBNIZ

The best index to a person's character is
    (1) how he treats people who
        can't do him any good, and
    (2) how he treats people who
        can't fight back.

ABIGAIL VAN BUREN

The world is moved along, not only
by the mighty shoves of its heroes,
but also by the aggregate of the
tiny pushes of each honest worker.

HELEN KELLER

Believe that life is worth living,
and your belief will help create the fact.

HENRY JAMES

Be glad of life because it gives
you the chance to love, to work, to play,
and to look up at the stars.

Henry van Dyke

Let all that you do be done in love.

1 CORINTHIANS 16:14 NRSV

Love is of utmost importance.
Once you have set your will that you
will learn the way of love,
then there is no flaw or irritation
in another person that you cannot bear.

TERESA OF AVILA

Love. . .is an ever-fixed mark
that looks on tempests and is never shaken.

WILLIAM SHAKESPEARE

You learn to like someone when you
find out what makes them laugh,
but you can never truly love someone
until you find out what makes them cry.

UNKNOWN

The greatest use of life is to spend it
for something that will outlast it.

WILLIAM JAMES

It is in our lives and not our words
that our religion must be read.

THOMAS JEFFERSON

A life with love will have some thorns,
but a life without love will have no roses.

UNKNOWN

A successful relationship comes not
so much from finding the right partner,
but rather from being the right partner and
demonstrating love, faith, hope, and forgiveness.

UNKNOWN

[Love] makes everything that is heavy light,
and it bears evenly all that is uneven.

THOMAS À KEMPIS

Worry gives a small thing a big shadow.

SWEDISH PROVERB

Have genuine mutual love,
love one another deeply from the heart.

1 PETER 1:22 NRSV

Immature love says,
"I love you because I need you."
Mature love says,
"I need you because I love you."

ERICH FROMM

Young love is a flame; very pretty, often very hot
and fierce, but still only light and flickering.
The love of the older and disciplined heart
is as coals, deep burning, unquenchable.

HENRY WARD BEECHER

Love creates an "us"
without destroying a "me."

UNKNOWN

This is the true measure of love,
when we believe that we alone can love,
that no one could ever have loved so before us,
and that no one will ever
love in the same way after us.

JOHANN WOLFGANG VON GOETHE

Have a heart that never hardens,
and a temper that never tires,
and a touch that never hurts.

CHARLES DICKENS

A good deed is never lost. . . .
He who plants kindness gathers love.

BASIL

No snowflake in an avalanche ever feels responsible.

VOLTAIRE

Equality is the firmest bond of love.

GOTTHOLD EPHRAIM LESSING

We find rest in those we love,
and we provide a resting place in
ourselves for those who love us.

BERNARD OF CLAIRVAUX

Love has no age, as it is always renewing.

BLAISE PASCAL

[Love] always protects, always trusts,
always hopes, always perseveres.

1 CORINTHIANS 13:7 NIV

Where love reigns,
the very joy of heaven itself is felt.

HANNAH HURNARD

When the heart is pure it cannot
help loving, because it has discovered
the source of love, which is God.

JOHN VIANNEY

Love grows by giving.
The love we give away is the only love we keep.
The only way to retain love is to give it away.

Elbert Hubbard

A happy marriage is the union of two good forgivers.

ROBERT QUILLEN

The secret to a long marriage is to put a little romance in every day.

UNKNOWN